The toymaker's birthday

Kaye Umansky

M
MACMILLAN
EDUCATION

THE CAST

The Toymaker

Tom the Cat

Action Man

Toy Dog

Doll

Baby Doll

Teddy Bear

Captain of the
Toy Soldiers

Toy Soldiers

Ballerina Doll

Toy Rabbit

Rag Doll

First published 1986
Reprinted 1987

Published by
MACMILLAN EDUCATION LTD
Houndmills, Basingstoke,
Hampshire RG21 2XS
and London
Companies and representatives
throughout the world

Typeset by
Regent Typesetting, Odiham

Illustrated by Ken Morton

Printed in Hong Kong

British Library Cataloguing
in Publication Data
Umansky, Kaye
The toymaker's birthday. — (Playreaders)
I. Title   II. Series
428.6   PE1119
ISBN 0-333-39383-X

(The Toymaker is at his bench in the workshop. Tom is at his feet. Toys line the shelves. The clock strikes twelve.)

Toymaker:

Twelve o'clock already. Poor Tom, it's long past your supper time, isn't it?

Tom:

Meow.

Toymaker:

You're right. It's past my bedtime too.

Tom:

Meow, meow.

Toymaker:

I suppose you're right. I do work too hard at my age. But I so love making beautiful toys.

Tom:

Meow. Meow, meow.

Toymaker:

What, *tomorrow?* My birthday tomorrow? How old am I, Tom? Ah me. When I was young, I used to get presents on my birthday – but that was long, long ago. Now my only friends are my lovely toys.

Tom:

MEOW!

Toymaker:

Yes, of course. And you, Tom. Come on – let's get some supper. Goodnight, my toys. Sleep well.

SCENE 2

(The toys come alive.)

Action Man:

Who wants to sleep? Not me! I'm ready for action!

Dog:

Woof! Where did I bury that rubber bone?

Doll:

Ssh, Toy Dog, you'll wake the baby.

Baby Doll:
Mummy! Boohoo!

Doll:
There! See?

Captain:
Attention! Quick, march!

Soldiers:
Left, right, left, right!

Ballerina:
Must you march there, Captain? I want to dance and there isn't any room.

Action Man:
No dancing tonight. Or marching.

Soldiers:
No marching?

Ballerina:
No dancing? Why?

Action Man:
Because we're having a meeting.

Rabbit:
A meeting? What about?

Action Man:
Didn't you hear? Tomorrow is the Toymaker's birthday.

Dog:
Woof! So?

Action Man:
Well, what do Real People get on their birthdays?

All:

We don't know. What?

Action Man:

Presents, of course. And a cake.

Teddy:

Of course! We must give him presents. After all, he made us, didn't he?

Action Man:

We must all think very hard. Except for you, Rag Doll. You don't have a brain.

Rag Doll:

But I'd still like to give the Toymaker a present.

Doll:

Why? You're not a proper doll, like me.

Action Man:

He made you from left-over scraps.

Teddy:

Now, now, don't be unkind. Rag Doll can't help not being beautiful.

Action Man:

Everybody think. Who's got an idea?

Doll:

Baby Doll and I will bake him a cake in the toy cooker.

Captain:

We Soldiers will march down to the kitchen and get all the things Doll needs.

Ballerina:

I've got a good present. It's a silver thimble I found in a mousehole.

Dog:

Would he like my rubber bone?

All:

No!

Dog:

Then I'll give him the brass button I buried under the floorboards. He'll like that.

Rabbit:

I found an old pencil stub. I'll bite it sharp with my teeth. It'll be as good as new.

Teddy:

I can write, so I'll do the labels, and make him a birthday card. I shall need your pencil, Rabbit.

Action Man:

That just leaves me. I shall climb through the top window and pick a bunch of flowers from the blossom tree outside.

Teddy:

That's everybody, then.

Rag Doll:

No it isn't, there's me!

Doll:

We've already told you, Rag Doll. You don't count.

Rag Doll:

I want to give him a present. He made me too!

Ballerina:

I don't know why. He must have been very tired that night. Go away, Rag Doll. We're all very busy.

Captain:

Right, troops. Left, turn! To the kitchen, quick, march!

Soldiers:

Left, right, left, right . . .

(The Soldiers march out.)

Doll:

Get the aprons, Baby Doll.

Teddy:

Can I borrow the pencil?

Rabbit:

I'll get it.

Action Man:

Here I go then, up the curtains!

Dog:

Now, where did I bury that button?

(Enter Tom.)

Tom:

Meow.

Rag Doll:

Hallo, Tom.

Tom:

Meow?

Rag Doll:

No, I'm not crying – but I do feel sad.

Tom:

Meow?

Rag Doll:

Because all the toys are giving presents to the Toymaker for his birthday tomorrow, except me. They say I don't count. I'm just made from old scraps, you see.

Tom:

Meow! Meow, meow, meow!

Rag Doll:

You really think so? He'd *like* a present from me?

Tom:

Meow.

Rag Doll:

But what? I don't have anything to give.

Tom:

Meeeeooow.

Rag Doll:

Come behind the screen? What for?

Tom:

Meow, meow.

Rag Doll:

All right then. But I hope it's a *good* idea.

(Tom and Rag Doll go behind the screen.)

(Enter Soldiers.)

Soldiers:

Left, right, left, right . . .

Captain:

Halt! Here you are, Doll. Flour, sugar, eggs
– everything you need.

Doll:

Thank you. Is the bowl ready, Baby Doll?

Baby Doll:

Yes, Mummy.

Doll:

Then you can stir.

*(Tom comes from behind the screen with a length of
cotton in his mouth. Teddy trips over it.)*

Teddy:

Hey! What are you doing, Tom?

Tom:

Meow.

Action Man:

What's all this cotton?

Tom:

Meow.

Rabbit:

What do you mean, a secret? You're tripping everyone up!

Ballerina:

What's happening?

Dog:

Tom's pulling cotton everywhere.

Action Man:

Oh, leave him alone, silly cat. We've got too much to do to worry about him. It'll soon be daybreak.

(The next morning. Enter Tom, tugging the Toymaker. The Toys are back on the shelves.)

Toymaker:

All right, Tom, I'm coming.

Tom:

Meow, meow.

Toymaker:

A surprise, you say? But – Oh! What's all this?

Tom:

Meow, meow.

Toymaker:

Birthday presents? For *me?* But who from?

Tom:

Meow, meow.

Toymaker:

The *toys*? Well, I never did! Why, look! It's a birthday cake! It says: 'From Doll, Baby Doll and the Soldiers.'

Tom:

Meow.

Toymaker:

What's this? A card! 'For Toymaker, with
love from Teddy'. Oh, Teddy! And – why, a
thimble from Ballerina – and here's a
beautifully sharp pencil from Rabbit. Just
what I wanted. Oh, and a shiny button from
Dog – and a bunch of flowers from Action
Man. I just don't know what to say. Thank
you, Toys, thank you so much.

Tom:

MEOW! MEOW!

Toymaker:

The floor? What about it? Why, what's all
this cotton doing on the floor?

Tom:

Meow, meow.

Toymaker:

You're right! It does spell something.
'Happy Birthday, from Rag Doll.' Oh, even
my dear little Rag Doll remembered me. But
where is she?

Tom:

Meow, meow.

Toymaker:

Behind the screen? What's she doing there?

(The Toymaker goes to the screen.)

Toymaker:

Oh no! She's unstitched herself, and used her cotton for the writing. I suppose she didn't have anything else to give me. Never mind, little friend. I shall sew you up again tonight, and you'll be as good as new. You always were one of my favourites – and you've given me the best birthday present I ever had!

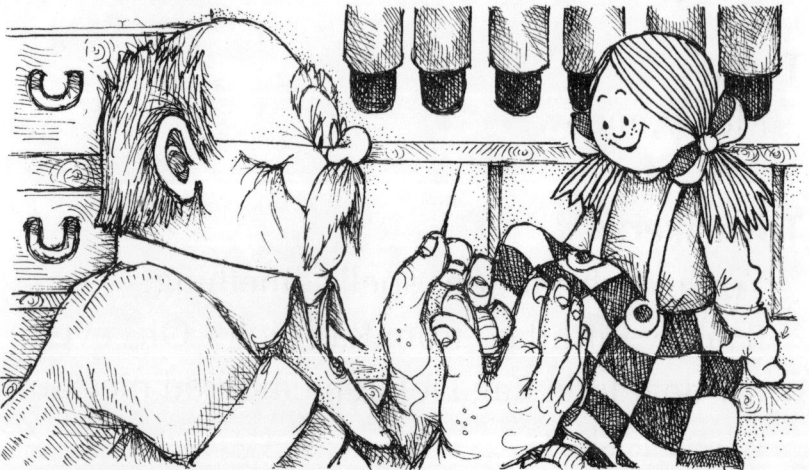